8/10

MYTHS FROM AROUND THE WORLD

MESOAMERICAN MYTHS

By Anita Dalal

Gareth Stevens
Publishing

Please visit our Web site www.garethstevens.com. For a free color catalog of all our high-quality books, call toll free 1-800-542-2595 or fax 1-877-542-2596.

Library of Congress Cataloging-in-Publication Data
Dalal, Anita.
    Mesoamerican myths / Anita Dalal.
       p. cm. — (Myths from around the world)
    Includes index.
    ISBN 978-1-4339-3539-8 (library binding) — ISBN 978-1-4339-3540-4 (pbk.)
    ISBN 978-1-4339-3541-1 (library binding)
     1. Aztec mythology—Juvenile literature. 2. Maya mythology—Juvenile literature.
     3. Inca mythology—Juvenile literature. I. Title.
   F1219.76.R45D348 2010
   299.7'8452—dc22   2009037157

Published in 2010 by
Gareth Stevens Publishing
111 East 14th Street, Suite 349
New York, NY 10003

© 2010 The Brown Reference Group Ltd.

For Gareth Stevens Publishing:
Art Direction: Haley Harasymiw
Editorial Direction: Kerri O'Donnell

For The Brown Reference Group Ltd:
Editorial Director: Lindsey Lowe
Managing Editor: Tim Cooke
Editor: Henry Russell
Children's Publisher: Anne O'Daly
Picture Manager: Sophie Mortimer
Design Manager: David Poole
Designers: Tim Mayer and John Walker
Production Director: Alastair Gourlay

Picture Credits:
Front Cover: Jupiter Images: Photos.com b; Stockxpert t, m

iStock: Bobbidog 37; Jupiter Images: Photos.com 17t, 32, 33t, 33b, 36, 43, 44, 45; Shutterstock: 5, 13, 15, 27; Danilo Ascione 35; Joel Bilt 12; Karla Caspari 9t; Martin Dallaire 24; Bill Frische 8; Gordon Galbraith 7; Amy Nichole Harris 17b; Georgios Kollidas 40; Grigory Kubatyan 41; Lagui 28; Modestlife 20; Nicholas Raymond 18; Dmitry Rukhlenko 8b; Carlos E. Santa Maria 21; W. Scott 16; Dwight Smith 39; John Sones 29; Jef Thompson 23; Andrew Tichovolsky 25t; Underworld 11; Wheeler Images 31

Publisher's note to educators and parents: Our editors have carefully reviewed the Web sites that appear on p. 47 to ensure that they are suitable for students. Many Web sites change frequently, however, and we cannot guarantee that a site's future contents will continue to meet our high standards of quality and educational value. Be advised that students should be closely supervised whenever they access the Internet.

Manufactured in the United States of America
1 2 3 4 5 6 7 8 9 12 11 10

CPSIA compliance information: Batch #BRW0102GS: For further information contact Gareth Stevens, New York, New York at 1-800-542-2595.

Contents

Introduction 4

The Creation of the Earth 6

Cultures and Empires 8

The Creation of Corn People 10

Agriculture in Mesoamerica 12

Coniraya Viracocha 14

The Shape of Inca Society 16

The Origin of Cuzco 18

Capital of the Inca 20

The Ball Game in the Underworld 22

The Sacred Ball Game 24

Vucub Caquix Battles the Twins 26

Mayan Life and Myths 28

The Birth of Huitzilopochtli 30

Huitzilopochtli's Temple 32

Tezcatlipoca's Revenge 34

Gods and Sacrifice 36

The Five Suns 38

Aztec Calendars 40

The Departure of Quetzalcoatl 42

The Fall of the Aztec Empire 44

Glossary and Further Information 46

Index 48

Introduction

Myths are mirrors of humanity. They reflect the soul of a culture and try to give profound answers in a seemingly mysterious world. They give people an understanding of their place in the world and the universe.

Found in all civilizations, myths sometimes combine fact and fiction and at other times are complete fantasy.

Every culture has its own myths. Yet, globally, there are common themes, even across civilizations that had no contact with each other. The most common myths deal with the creation of the world or of a particular site, like a mountain or a lake. Other myths deal with the origin of humans or describe the heroes and gods who either made the world inhabitable or who provided humans with something essential, such as the ancient Greek Titan Prometheus, who gave fire, and the Native American Ojibwa hero Wunzh, who was given divine instructions on cultivating corn. There are also myths about the end of the world, death and the afterlife, and the seasons.

The origin of evil and death are also common themes. Examples of such myths are the Biblical Eve eating the forbidden fruit and the ancient Greek story of Pandora opening the sealed box. There are also flood myths, myths about the sun and the moon, and myths of peaceful places of reward, such as heaven or Elysium, and of places of punishment, such as hell or Tartarus. Myths also teach human values, such as honesty.

This book deals with the myths of the pre-Columbian cultures of America. Following each myth is an explanation of how the myth related to the real life of the particular civilization. A glossary at the end of the book identifies the major mythological and historical characters, and explains many cultural terms.

Pre-Columbian Mythology

Pre-Columbian cultures are those that originated in Mexico, Central America, and the Andes of South America before the Spanish conquered the New World in the 16th century. For thousands of years, the Mixtecs, Olmecs, and Teotihuacans built large cities and practiced highly

The Aztecs decorated the stone walls of their most important buildings with intricate carvings.

structured rituals related to sacred myths. These achievements and practices were later adopted by the empires of the Incas in the Andes and the Aztecs and Mayas in Mexico and Central America.

As in many cultures, the myths of the pre-Columbian peoples reflected their civilization. The Aztecs, for example, believed that their gods would favor them in war only if they were offered blood, so they practiced ritual human sacrifice.

Meanwhile, these sometimes violent cultures made great advances in art and science. They produced complex calendars and developed their own hieroglyphics (picture words). The Spanish conquerors were amazed by their achievements.

The Creation of the Earth

The peoples of pre-Columbian America, like most ancient cultures, viewed their surroundings as both life-sustaining and destructive. The theme of this Aztec creation myth is typical of the region — out of conflict comes good.

At the beginning of time there existed only the earth and the sky. The surface of the earth was covered in water, and the only creatures that dwelled there were monsters. The sky was the home of the gods, who had very unpredictable relationships with each other. Sometimes they worked together to defeat monsters or create worlds, at other times they tried to destroy each other and all that existed.

One day, two gods, Tezcatlipoca and Quetzalcoatl, were looking down on the earth when they saw a huge alligator-like monster swimming on the surface of the water. To get a closer look, the two gods flew down low. As they approached the creature, they saw that it was Tlaltecuhtli, a greedy she-monster with an insatiable appetite. Tlaltecuhtli not only had a very large mouth full of sharp teeth in her face, but also many other mouths all over her body, including on her feet and knees and running all the way up to her elbows and hands. Having so many mouths meant that Tlaltecuhtli could eat anything in or above the water.

Changing Shapes

Tezcatlipoca and Quetzalcoatl wanted to create dry land on the earth's surface, but they had to work out a way to stop Tlaltecuhtli from devouring it. The two gods turned themselves into two giant serpents and dove into the water to look for the hungry Tlaltecuhtli.

When they found Tlaltecuhtli, one of the serpent gods grabbed her left hand and right foot and the other serpent god took hold of the monster's right hand and left foot. Between them they pulled harder and harder until the monster began to split in two. The lower half of Tlaltecuhtli's body rose to form the heavens high above the sky, the top part of her body fell to form the land, and her spiny back became the earth's mountains.

The other gods in the sky did not want dry land on earth. When they saw what Tezcatlipoca and Quetzalcoatl had done to Tlaltecuhtli, they became very angry. So to appease the other gods, Tezcatlipoca and Quetzalcoatl quickly decided that they would use what was left of Tlaltecuhtli's body to make the rest of nature for living creatures to inhabit.

From Tlaltecuhtli's hair, the two gods made all the trees, flowers, and herbs. From her skin, they made all the grasses and flowers. The monster's eyes became the source of wells and springs. Her many mouths were turned into great rivers and caverns. Her nose was transformed into gentle hills and valleys.

When Tezcatlipoca and Quetzalcoatl had finished their creation, the other gods were very pleased with the result and forgave the two gods for transforming Tlaltecuhtli.

Quetzalcoatl was one of the most popular Aztec gods. This mask is mounted on the wall of his temple in Teotihuacan, Mexico.

Cultures and Empires

The Mayas, Aztecs, and Incas developed rich and varied civilizations. Their achievements ranged from architectural and economic innovations to military and cultural conquests.

The Mayas were highly accomplished artists. This is a Mayan death mask.

When the Spanish arrived in America, they discovered three major cultures: the Mayas, the Aztecs, and the Incas.

The Mayas and the Aztecs were influenced by the earlier local cultures of the Olmecs and the Toltecs, who excelled in art and architecture and had complex social systems.

The Olmecs, who lived in southern Mexico, were dominant between 1100 and 800 B.C. They built ball courts, pyramids, and city squares, and developed hieroglyphic writing (using pictures to signify words).

The Toltecs ruled central Mexico for over 300 years from A.D. 900. Their artists left many sculptures showing their war victories against rivals such as the Mixtecs.

The Mayas, who lived in the Yucatán peninsula of present-day Mexico, developed a civilization that lasted from 1000 B.C. until the Spanish conquest in the early sixteenth century. Although they had no capital city, the Mayas spread a common culture over a large area. They were expert astronomers and mathematicians. They invented their own hieroglyphic writing and produced codices

(illustrated books), four of which still exist today. These codices contain information about the Mayan gods, many of which were the same as the gods worshipped by the Aztecs but with different names.

Rise of the Aztecs and the Incas

The Aztecs were a wandering tribe before they settled in Mexico and founded Tenochtitlán, their capital city, in around 1325. For two centuries the Aztecs dominated the area until their rule was ended by the Spanish.

A dancer at the May Day Parade in Minneapolis, Minnesota, wears a traditional Aztec headdress.

The Aztecs demanded labor from the people they conquered but they also respected their cultures and often integrated the gods of others into their own religion. The main Aztec gods included Tlaloc, the god of rain, who may have been Olmec in origin, and Quetzalcoatl, who was often represented as a plumed serpent and was derived from Toltec mythology. Huitzilopochtli, the god of war, was an entirely Aztec creation and may have actually been an ancient Aztec leader.

From the early fifteenth century until the early sixteenth century, the Incas controlled an empire that stretched along the Pacific coast of South America from Ecuador to central Chile and included an estimated 12 million people. They had a capital city, Cuzco, founded in the 12th century, and ruled their vast empire through a network of roads and bridges.

The Pyramid of the Sun in Teotihuacan, Mexico, is one of the greatest architectural achievements of the Mesoamerican civilizations.

The Creation of Corn People

Agriculture—especially growing corn—was basic to the survival of pre-Columbian cultures. It was so important that this Mayan myth describes corn people as the ancestors of humans.

At the start of the world people did not exist. There were no animals of any kind, no grass, no flowers, and no trees. There was nothing more than the sky, the oceans, the earth, and the gods.

Lying coiled at the bottom of the sea was the god Gucumatz, a plumed serpent. High in the sky was the god Huracan, also called Heart of Heaven, who appeared with bolts of lightning shooting from his head. Together the two gods discussed how they might create a world. As they talked, mountains began to rise from the sea and forests covered the earth, just as they described.

The gods decided to put animals on the land. They asked the animals to pray and give thanks to their creators, but the animals could not speak. They could only squawk and make howling noises. So the gods decided to invent a creature that would rule over the animals and would praise the gods properly and feed them with offerings.

Human Creation

The creature they decided to make was a man. The first man was made from clay. He could speak, but only nonsense. His body was so weak that it started to crumble and dissolve. The gods broke him apart and started again. This time they made a man out of wood, and before they knew it the world was full of wooden men.

The wooden men could speak, but they were rude and lacked feelings. Worse still, they were not grateful to their creators and refused to pray to them. The wooden men were so mean that even their own

This ancient sculpture is thought to represent one of the many gods of the Mayan civilization. The figure is wearing ceremonial dress.

cooking pots and animals turned against them. The gods decided to destroy them. They sent a huge flood to wash them away. The wooden men tried to escape the rising waters but failed.

After the flood, the earth still had no creatures to rule over the animals. Seeking advice from other gods, Huracan and Gucumatz decided to make new men out of corn. They made four who were unlike any of the earlier men.

The corn men were highly intelligent and very grateful to their creators, but the gods were afraid that the corn men were too clever. So the gods decided to take away some of the corn men's wisdom and replace it with happiness in the form of four corn women. It is from the four corn men and four corn women that the whole of the human race is descended.

Agriculture in Mesoamerica

In pre-Columbian society, the most common occupation was farming. The way pre-Columbian farmers worked varied from region to region according to the nature of the landscape.

Mesoamerica is the area between modern central Mexico and Honduras and Nicaragua. Pre-Columbian inhabitants of this region lived in small villages where they grew corn, beans, squashes, chili peppers, and cotton. Of these crops, corn proved the most dependable and versatile.

To store harvested corn, Mesoamericans mixed ripe kernels with water and white lime to make a preservative. This process, known as mixtamal, enabled corn to be stored and later ground for tamales and tortillas.

Although the warm climate made growing corn easy, there were some problems. The crop could be farmed for only a few years on the same patch of land before it depleted the soil's nutrients. To prevent this,

Many Incas built farms on terraces that they carved out of steep hillsides. This typical example lies on the shores of Lake Titicaca in Bolivia.

Many Mesoamerican buildings were built in jungle clearings. Neglected after the Spanish conquest of the region, many of them disappeared under thick vegetation. The sites were cleared again in the twentieth century.

FLOATING GARDENS

The Aztecs' method of farming was unusual in Mesoamerica. They farmed on floating gardens. In a unique feat of engineering, the Aztecs reclaimed the swamp land on Lake Texcoco on which their capital, Tenochtitlán, was founded, and placed flat reeds on top of the marshland. They then covered the platforms with soil and on them produced abundant crops.

Mesoamerican farmers practiced crop rotation and planted secondary crops, such as beans and squashes, along with corn, to replenish the soil.

In Yucatán, Mayas carved out farm land from the tropical rain forest. They did this by slash-and-burn farming, cutting down forests, burning trees, and planting seed on the cleared land. The soil produced was usually of poor quality, and only two to four years of farming were possible. For Mayas who lived at higher elevations, the land was of better quality and could be farmed for about 10 years.

Inca Terrace Farming

In South America, methods of farming were very different from those used in Mesoamerica. Some inhabitants of the Inca empire lived on the steep slopes of the Andes. In these high-altitude areas potato, not corn, was the primary crop.

To make the mountainous terrain suitable for cultivation, Inca farmers practiced terrace farming by cutting out level terraces that appear like giant steps running up the side of a mountain. The terraces retained water and prevented fertile soil from washing away.

Coniraya Viracocha

The spirit Coniraya Viracocha was at times mischievous.
He even pretended to be the mighty Viracocha, who the
Incas believed was the force behind all creation.

At a time not long after the creation of people, the earth was still populated by nature spirits. There were also animals, but they had not yet been given all their characteristics. It was during this era that the spirit Coniraya Viracocha decided to wander the earth disguised as a beggar to interact with people.

One day a beautiful woman, Cavillaca, sat weaving beneath a tree. She had many admirers but lived alone. Passing by, Coniraya Viracocha saw her and immediately fell in love. He turned himself into a bird and flew into the tree to be near her. Cavillaca loved the tree's fruit and ate some of it. When she ate the fruit that Coniraya had touched, it made her pregnant.

The child Cavillaca bore was a boy, and on his first birthday she summoned all the men of her village to find out who the father was. The men came dressed in their best clothes, but no one admitted to being the father. Cavillaca decided to put the baby on the floor and see who he would crawl to.

Coniraya, dressed only in rags, tried to hide quietly in a corner, but the baby crawled straight to him. Cavillaca was furious when she realized that a scruffy beggar was the father of her baby. In her anger, she took the child and fled.

Giving Chase

When Coniraya heard that Cavillaca had left, he rushed after her. On his way he met a condor, who told the spirit that he would soon catch Cavillaca. To show his thanks, Coniraya blessed the condor with the power to fly above mountains and to nest where it would be safe.

Next Coniraya met a fox, who said Cavillaca was so far away that he would never catch her. Coniraya cursed the animal so that it would always be unloved.

Finally, he met some macaws, who told him he was too late—Cavillaca and her baby had turned into rocks the moment

Coniraya condemned macaws to chatter noisily so that they could never hide from predators.

they reached the sea. Although this was the truth, Coniraya cursed the macaws by making them sing so loudly that they would always be heard by their predators.

When Coniraya finally got to the coast he found the rocks that had once been Cavillaca and her baby. He was so angry that he tipped the fish from a local goddess's pond into the sea. From these fish come all the fish in the sea. The goddess was furious and tried to kill Coniraya, but he managed to escape.

The Shape of Inca Society

At its height, the Inca empire was the largest in South America, governing an estimated 12 million people. The rulers were able to maintain order only because of their firmly structured society.

Inca society was very inflexible. Whatever social position a person was born into was the one in which he or she remained. This helps to explain why the people in the myth did not recognize Coniraya Viracocha when he was dressed in old rags—spirits were supposed to wear finer clothes.

At the top of Inca society was the ruler of the empire, who called himself the Inca. He was considered to be a direct descendant of the creator, a being known as Viracocha, a deity adopted from pre-Inca civilizations. The Inca ruler was also thought to be the human representative of Viracocha, making his position and power absolute. Directly below the Inca ruler was the royal family.

Next in importance were the priests and nobles. Together, these top layers of the society made up the aristocracy. The ordinary members of the Inca empire were at the bottom of the hierarchy.

This sculpted figurine was carved by Incas in around 100 B.C.

Every member of Inca society belonged to an ayllu, or social group. The ayllus formed the basis of Inca government.

The imperial administration and religious posts were filled by noblemen and priests from the royal ayllu. Working for them were the regional ayllu chiefs, who organized the payment of mita.

Paying Inca Tax

Mita was a tax that was paid in the form of goods such as weapons, cloth, wool, potatoes, and corn. Ordinary members of the Inca empire, excluding

Atahualpa was the last emperor of the Incas.

Machu Picchu, in modern Peru, was one of the main Inca centers.

the aristocracy, were expected to divide their land and goods into three parts. One third of the land was given to the emperor and state, another third to the priests, gods, and sun, and the final third to the local ayllu. By dividing land and goods three ways, the emperor was able to increase his own wealth and keep in check his conquered people, who were left with nothing for themselves.

The ayllu was such a dominant part of people's lives that the notion of individual freedom did not exist. This caused great dissatisfaction among the peasants, whose language contained many words for unhappiness.

The Origin of Cuzco

About 15 miles (24 km) from Cuzco, the Inca capital, is Mount Paqaritampu. In the cliff face there are three caves, and it is from the middle cave that the Incas believed the founders of their royal dynasty emerged.

One day, many centuries ago, four brothers and their four sisters came out of a cave on Paqaritampu. They all dressed very differently from the local people who lived alongside the mountain. The creator god Viracocha had told the siblings to set off on foot and look for a site on which to build a city.

As they climbed the mountains that surround Paqaritampu, the eldest brother, Ayar Cachi, whose name means "salt," started to show off. At the top of a mountain called Huanacauri, in a village of the same name, Ayar Cachi took out his sling and started to hurl stones. He was so strong that, as the stones hit the neighboring hills, their force caused ravines to appear. His brothers were extremely angry with Ayar Cachi for showing off and so devised a plan to punish him.

They persuaded him to return to the cave. When he stepped inside, they quickly walled up the entrance, trapping him. The others then continued on their journey, but the second brother, Ayar Ucho, whose name means "pepper," decided to stay in the village of Huanacauri. He turned himself into stone so that he might become immortal and be worshipped as a shrine. The third brother, Ayar Sauca, whose name means "joy," also decided that he did not want to continue the search for a site for the new city. Instead, he chose to live with the peasants and become a spirit of the fields.

Founding the Inca Capital

This left only one brother, Ayar Manco, and his four sisters who continued on their quest until they reached a spot miles from where they had started. Mama Ocllo, one of the sisters, said, "Let's build our capital city here." Using a gold stick they had brought with them on the journey, they tapped the ground to discover where the exact center of the city should be. Then Ayar Manco, who from then on was

known as Manco Capac, married his sister, Mama Ocllo. Together they became the first Inca rulers.

They set about building the beautiful city, which they called Cuzco, intending that it should reflect the glory of Viracocha. In his honor, they built a temple and many magnificent palaces. Manco Capac, Mama Ocllo, and the nobles of the Inca empire would live in Cuzco for many years.

Cuzco, the former Inca capital, is still one of the largest and busiest cities in modern Peru. It is located high in the Andes Mountains.

19

Capital of the Inca

The capital of the Inca empire, Cuzco was a splendid city built with amazing engineering. Little of the original city remains, however, having been built over by the Spanish.

Manco Capac and Mama Ocllo were real people who founded Cuzco and the Inca royal dynasty in the twelfth century A.D. During the reign of Pachacuti, in the fifteenth century, the Incas expanded their territory by conquering neighboring cultures. It was during this period that Cuzco became the center of the Inca empire. Pachacuti himself oversaw the redevelopment of the capital.

Cuzco, which means "navel" or "center" in the Quechua language, lies in a valley at a height of 11,500 feet (3,500 m). Pachacuti turned two local rivers into canals and built a ceremonial square over one of them at the center of the city.

The city was planned to resemble the shape of a puma, because the Incas considered the big cat a symbol of strength. A fortress that protected the center was located at the puma's head, and at the puma's tail the two canals merged. Within the animal shape, the

The stones in this wall in Cuzco fit together so tightly without cement that there is no danger of dislodging any of them.

city was arranged in a grid, with the narrow paved streets crossing each other at right angles, just like in many modern American cities. The central part was also divided into four sections to represent the four corners of the empire.

Building the Capital

It took 50,000 craftsmen and builders 20 years to create the imperial city. The streets had stone gutters for drainage, and the buildings were made out of hard volcanic rock that workmen cut carefully into large blocks and then fitted tightly together without mortar. The blocks interlocked so exactly that it is impossible to slip a piece of paper between them.

The heart of ancient Cuzco was the ceremonial square. Four main streets led off the square, one to each corner of the empire. People resided in the district that matched their place of origin, so someone from the east of the empire would live in the east of the city.

Only the Inca (the ruler), high-ranking nobles, and conquered chieftains could live in the heart of the capital. People of lower social rank had to live in the outskirts.

Within Cuzco was the most sacred place in the Inca empire, the Temple of the Sun. Today, a curved wall of the temple survives intact, although most of it was covered by a Spanish church.

Above: This map shows the Inca empire just before the Spanish arrived.

This beautiful jar was made by South Americans who lived in Peru before the rise of the Inca civilization in the twelfth century.

The Ball Game in the Underworld

The ball game tlachtli was popular across Mesoamerica. For the Mayas, the ball game was so important that two of their most revered mythological characters were expert players.

The twin brothers Hunhun-Ahpu and Vukub-Ahpu were the world's best players of the ball game tlachtli. The lords of the underworld kingdom of Xibalba were also good players and challenged the twins to a game.

When the twins descended into Xibalba, they found that they had been tricked. They would first have to overcome a series of obstacles before even reaching the ball court. The brothers failed at the obstacles, and the evil lords had them put to death.

Their bodies were buried, but the head of Hunhun-Ahpu was hung in a tree in Xibalba as a trophy. Until that day the tree had never borne any fruit, but immediately afterward its branches were full. The lords then forbade anyone to touch the tree.

Revenge Match

One day, a curious young girl named Xquiq could not resist plucking the fruit. As she stretched out her hand, the head of Hunhun-Ahpu spat on her palm. "Quick," the head told her, "hurry to the upperworld where you will bear my sons." The girl was scared but fled Xibalba with the evil lords in hot pursuit.

Having reached the upperworld, Xquiq gave birth to twin sons, whom she named Hunahpu and Xbalanque. The twins grew up to become great players of tlachtli.

The lords challenged Hunahpu and Xbalanque to a game of tlachtli, and the twins descended into Xibalba, just as their father and uncle had done. Unlike them, however, the twins knew that the lords would try to trick them. They overcame the challenges and, when they finally

This Mayan ball player appears on numerous Mesoamerican pottery designs and on the walls of several pre-Columbian temples.

got to play the game, they won it.

The evil lords then forced the twins to go through another series of challenges, but the brothers set a trap of their own. They pretended to lose and allowed the lords to burn them on a funeral pyre. Their ashes were scattered, but five days later two strange figures—half-men, half-fish—appeared. The new creatures performed tricks, burning and then remaking animals.

Impressed, the lords of Xibalba asked the figures to burn them as well. As the lords disappeared into the flames, the brothers threw off their disguises and shouted that the evil lords would not be re-created.

The Sacred Ball Game

Each Mesoamerican group had its own variation of tlachtli and treated the winners and losers differently. Some groups sacrificed the winners, other groups killed the losers.

Throughout Mesoamerica, wherever there was a religious temple there was usually a sacred ball court nearby. The ball court was used to play the game of tlachtli.

The origins of tlachtli are uncertain but it may have been developed by the ancient Olmecs. It later became an important part of Mayan and other Mesoamerican cultures, as the myth of Hunahpu and Xbalanque shows.

In some ways, the ball game was an early predecessor of modern basketball and soccer. A typical court was shaped like the capital letter "H" and was oriented either east-to-west or north-to-south. The court was usually enclosed by high stone walls on which were carved sculptures of gods and demons.

The object of the game was to get a solid rubber ball through one of two stone hoops placed opposite each other high on the court walls. The difficulty was that the players of the two opposing teams could

The magnificent ball court in Coba, Mexico, is one of the best preserved Mayan tlachtli arenas in Mesoamerica.

not use their feet or hands. Instead they had to use their elbows, knees, or hips, which were all protected with padding.

Religious Meaning

Some archaeologists believe that the court represented heaven and the ball the sun, the moon, or the stars. The

This photograph shows part of the ball court at Chichén Itzá as it looks today.

hoops symbolized sunrise or sunset, or perhaps the fall and spring equinoxes (when daytime and nighttime are of equal length).

In keeping with the religious importance of the game, it is believed that, in Mayan society, the captain of the winning team was sacrificed to the gods. In Aztec society, however, it is thought that it was the losing player who was sacrificed so that his life would give birth to the new sun.

In Aztec society, only nobles were allowed to play tlachtli, but the game was enjoyed by spectators of all classes, who would place bets on the outcome.

THE GRAND BALL COURT AT CHICHÉN ITZÁ

The ball court at the Mayan city of Chichén Itzá, which was controlled by the Toltecs from the tenth century to the late twelfth century, is the largest and grandest ever found in Mesoamerica. At both long ends of the ball court lie two small temples, with the one at the north end housing many fine stone reliefs depicting Toltec culture. On top of the east wall of the ball court is another temple that has frescoes of the Toltec invasion of the Mayan territories in the Yucatán.

Vucub Caquix Battles the Twins

The heavenly twins are prominent in several important Mayan myths that feature in the Popol Vuh, a famous book of Mayan mythology written in the sixteenth century.

Before the creation of humans, a boastful bird god called Vucub Caquix pretended he was the sun, the moon, and the light. Offended by his arrogance, the heavenly twins, Hunahpu and Xbalanque, declared war on him.

The heavenly twins knew that Vucub Caquix liked to eat the fruit of a particular tree, so they lay in wait nearby. When the bird god appeared for his daily meal, they fired arrows and wounded him. The bird god fought with the heavenly twins. Vucub Caquix pulled off one of Hunahpu's arms and made off with it.

To retrieve the arm, the twins got a crafty old man and his wife to help. The old couple went in search of Vucub Caquix and found him suffering from toothache and sore eyes. They convinced him that they could heal his ailments.

First, the crafty old couple pulled out all the bird god's teeth and replaced them with sharp grains of corn. Then they gorged out the bird god's eyes. Vucub Caquix had now lost all his power and his sight, and he could not stop the crafty old couple from seizing Hunahpu's severed arm. When the old couple took the severed arm to Hunahpu, the heavenly twin easily fixed it back in place.

Comeback

But the battle was not yet over. Vucub Caquix had two sons—Zipacna and Cabraca—who were determined to carry on their father's fight against the twins. One day, Zipacna came across 400 warriors who were trying to carry a giant log to prop up the roof of their enormous house. He offered to help and was so

strong that he
carried the giant log
all on his own. He did not know
that the warriors were allies of the heavenly twins. Recognizing Zipacna, they
devised a plan to destroy him.

After Zipacna had delivered the giant
log, they coaxed him into a deep pit and
buried him. Zipacna realized that it was a
trap but played along by pretending to be
dead. Believing they had killed him, the
warriors returned to their house to
celebrate. Zipacna then quietly snuck up
to the warriors' house and killed them all.

To avenge the warriors' deaths, the
heavenly twins made a model of a large
and very tasty crab, which they used to
lure Zipacna to a mountain cave. When he

**Some art historians
believe that this Mayan
sculpture represents the bird
god Vucub Caquix.**

was about to eat the crab, the mountain
fell on top of him.

Next the twins took Zipacna's brother,
Cabraca, hunting and fed him the birds
they had caught. Cabraca did not know
that the food was poisoned and died after
only a few bites.

With the defeat of Vucub Caquix and
his two sons, the world was finally safe
enough for Hunahpu and Xbalanque to
create humans.

Mayan Life and Myths

The Mayas painted their mythological characters on walls and ceramics and told of their exploits in texts known as codices, using picture-words called hieroglyphics.

The story of Hunahpu and Xbalanque's fight with Vucub Caquix can be found in the sacred Mayan book, the *Popol Vuh*. The *Popol Vuh*, which dates from the mid-sixteenth century, was written by Mayan scribes in their own language but used Spanish letters. The stories tell of the battles of the gods and their attempts to create a creature—man— that would be able to worship its creator.

The *Popol Vuh* is an excellent source for anyone who wants to learn more about the Mayas. Another essential source for researchers is a series of texts known as the codices. Only four Mayan codices exist, and three are named for the European cities where they are kept—Dresden, Madrid, and Paris. While the Dresden Codex is considered the finest and most complete, the Grolier Codex, which is the fourth and is held privately, is the oldest. It dates from A.D. 1230 and is the one most recently discovered by archaeologists, in 1971.

This ancient vase is one of the more recently discovered Mayan relics.

Deciphering a Culture

The codices were made out of folded strips of bark covered with gypsum gesso (made with glue and used for painting on). The writers used pens made from feathers that they dipped in red or black paint. With the pens they drew symbols that together form a story.

The translation of the symbols greatly increased

This map shows the Mayan civilization at its height.

historians' knowledge of Mayan culture. That knowledge continues to grow as archaeologists discover new sites and learn to decipher the symbols carved into the sides of buildings. Many Mayan sites were built in dense jungle, and over the centuries, trees and vegetation have overgrown the structures. As these sites are uncovered they reveal more about Mayan society.

Mayan mythology appears on many carvings on the sides of temples. For example, at Chichén Itzá's Temple of Jaguars, the adventures of the heavenly twins are recorded on the wall of the sacred ball court. At the ball court at Copán, a site in present-day Honduras, Vucub Caquix appears as a macaw.

One exciting Mayan discovery was Bonampak in the forest of the southern Mexican state of Chiapas. There, murals dating from before A.D. 800 were found that tell of a victorious Mayan battle and the victory celebrations that followed.

These Mayan ruins in Mexico were hidden for many years by vegetation.

The Birth of Huitzilopochtli

The battle between Huitzilopochtli and Coyolxauhqui is a myth of conflict, a common theme throughout the mythologies of Mesoamerica. Such conflicts came from observing nature, which can be both nurturing and destructive.

The goddess Coatlicue, also known as the Lady of the Serpent Skirt, was the mother of the Aztec gods. One day, when she was sweeping out the temple at Coatepec, a sacred mountain close to the ancient Toltec city of Tula, a ball of feathers floated to the ground. The feathers were very beautiful and Coatlicue picked them up. She tucked them into her waistband so that she could take them away with her. Later, when she got home and looked for the ball of feathers, it had disappeared. Unknown to Coatlicue, the feathers had special powers and they had made her pregnant with the mighty Huitzilopochtli, the god of war and sacrifice.

Coatlicue had already given birth to many gods, and as her womb grew larger, her sons wanted to know who the father of her unborn child was. When she could not give them a name, they told their warrior sister, Coyolxauhqui.

Child of Destiny

Coyolxauhqui was the leader of all her brothers and a strong and fearless fighter. She was very angry with their mother for getting pregnant without her permission and made sure that her brothers viewed their mother and the unborn child as enemies. She also convinced them that the only way to deal with the situation was to kill Coatlicue before she gave birth.

When Coatlicue found out what her children were planning she was very frightened, but the child growing inside her womb told her not to worry, saying, "Have no fear, already I know what I must do."

Soon afterward Coyolxauhqui and her brothers followed Coatlicue to the mountain of Coatepec, where they planned to kill her. The young gods rushed up the mountain in full battle dress, screaming their war cries. Just as they reached the top of the mountain and were ready to attack, Coatlicue gave birth to Huitzilopochtli. He emerged from his mother's belly fully grown and dressed as an armed warrior. In his hand was a burning weapon, a serpent of fire, known as Xiuhcoatl, or Turquoise Serpent.

The newborn Huitzilopochtli faced his warrior sister Coyolxauhqui in battle and with one swipe cut off her head. He then sliced her body into a hundred tiny pieces that tumbled down the mountainside.

When the others saw what the mighty Huitzilopochtli had done, they started to flee. But Huitzilopochtli chased his half-brothers around the mountain until he caught them. He killed many of them so that they could not harm Coatlicue but let a few of them escape to the south, after which they were never seen again.

This carved head of a serpent at Chichén Itzá in Mexico may depict the god Xiuhcoatl.

Huitzilopochtli's Temple

Tenochtitlán was a remarkable city built almost entirely on top of Lake Texcoco. It was also the most densely populated city in Mesoamerica, with an estimated 400,000 inhabitants.

These ancient building foundations were unearthed in Mexico City.

I n 1978 an electrical company digging in Mexico City made an exciting discovery. In the heart of the city they uncovered the ancient Aztec capital, Tenochtitlán, and the remains of the Great Pyramid, which was dedicated to Huitzilopochtli, the most important Aztec deity.

The only god to belong exclusively to the Aztecs—most of their gods were adopted from the cultures they had dominated—Huitzilopochtli, it was told, led the Aztecs to the site of their new city. There they found an eagle sitting on a cactus with a serpent in its beak. The eagle told the Aztecs that this was where they should build.

At the heart of the city was the Great Pyramid dedicated to Huitzilopochtli. It was used for all ceremonial events, including human sacrifice. One of the most important rituals was the inauguration of a new king.

On the death of a ruler, the heir to the throne withdrew from society. Dressed only in a loincloth, he was led by two noblemen to the bottom of the Great Pyramid. As a sign of humility the ruler-to-be was supported up the pyramid stairs by the noblemen to Huitzilopochtli's shrine.

There he was dressed in a dark green cape with skull-and-crossbones designs to represent his withdrawal from the present and a return to the dawn of time. Incense was burned in front of the shrine before the new ruler went down the stairs. The mood was somber among the watching crowd.

Four days of fasting followed for the new ruler, as he contemplated his new godlike role and carried out religious purification ceremonies. Meanwhile, a silent procession visited Huitzilopochtli's shrine each noon and midnight to burn incense.

These are some of the Aztec sculptures that were discovered in the Temple Mayor, Mexico City.

Crowning the New King

The coronation was a big contrast to the somber mood of the retreat. To assume his new position and mark his return to society, the ruler went to one of the royal palaces where he was dressed in the robes of state.

Finally, the king was carried on his throne to Huitzilopochtli's shrine at the top of the Great Pyramid, where he used a jaguar's claw to cut his skin and release some blood. Once he had offered his blood, more prayers and sermons followed and an offering of quail was made to cement the bond between the new ruler and the mighty Huitzilopochtli.

This Aztec skull rack was one of the most amazing of the 1978 discoveries in Mexico City.

Tezcatlipoca's Revenge

In Aztec mythology, the relationship between gods could change. Although they had worked together to create the earth (see page 6), Tezcatlipoca and Quetzalcoatl were also enemies.

The god Quetzalcoatl was very clever and very kind. He knew many things, such as where corn was hidden, the value of precious metals such as gold and silver, and the use of different plants. All this information he passed on to the Toltecs, who loved him greatly.

His popularity enraged the god Tezcatlipoca because it was he, not Quetzalcoatl, who had given life to humans. One day Tezcatlipoca visited Quetzalcoatl and held up a mirror. Quetzalcoatl saw in his reflection that he had become a wrinkled old man. Worried that his people would turn against him, Quetzalcoatl covered his face. Tezcatlipoca then persuaded him to look in the mirror again. This time Quetzalcoatl saw a handsome man. Now happy, he went back to his palace.

Tezcatlipoca, however, was not satisfied with just showing off his magical powers to Quetzalcoatl. He wanted to destroy him. The jealous god pretended to be Quetzalcoatl's friend. He offered him a special drink of pulque, a liquor made from the sap of the agave plant. At first Quetzalcoatl refused to taste the drink, but Tezcatlipoca kept offering it to him. Finally, Quetzalcoatl took a sip, and liking the taste, another and then another. Soon he was drunk. He asked his sister, Quetzalpetlatl, to drink with him and before long she too was drunk.

For a while, Quetzalcoatl and his sister lived a life of pleasure. Then, one day, they realized how irresponsible they were.

A Star Is Born

Quetzalcoatl was overcome with guilt. He ordered a stone coffin, and for four days he lay in it as a penance. Then, on the fifth day, he threw himself onto the flames of a funeral pyre. There was nothing anyone could do but, as his people watched helplessly, they noticed a new star burning brightly in the sky. Quetzalcoatl had become the morning star.

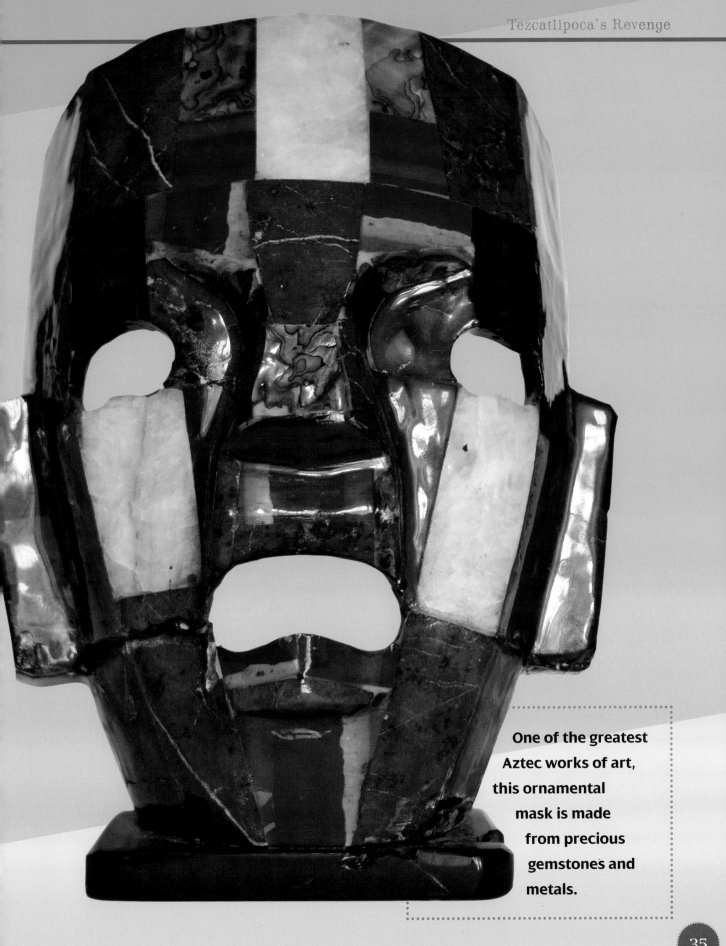

One of the greatest
Aztec works of art,
this ornamental
mask is made
from precious
gemstones and
metals.

Gods and Sacrifice

Ritual sacrifice was common in Mesoamerica, but the Aztecs took the practice to extremes, sometimes conducting series of human sacrifices lasting several days.

The Aztecs believed that order in society could be maintained only through warfare and human sacrifice. Wars became a regular event and even started on set dates. Between 1450 and 1519 there was a series of wars, known as the Wars of the Flowers, in which the Aztecs fought organized battles with warriors from other kingdoms.

The Aztecs fought wars not only to expand their empire but also to maintain a steady supply of victims for human sacrifice. They believed that the braver a captive was, the more nourishing he would be for the gods.

Range of Offerings

Prisoners of war were not the only ones to be sacrificed. Occasionally women and even Aztec warriors were fed to the gods. Indeed, Aztec soldiers believed that the two most honorable deaths were

This drawing shows sacrificial victims of the Aztecs being pushed down the steps of the sacred pyramid.

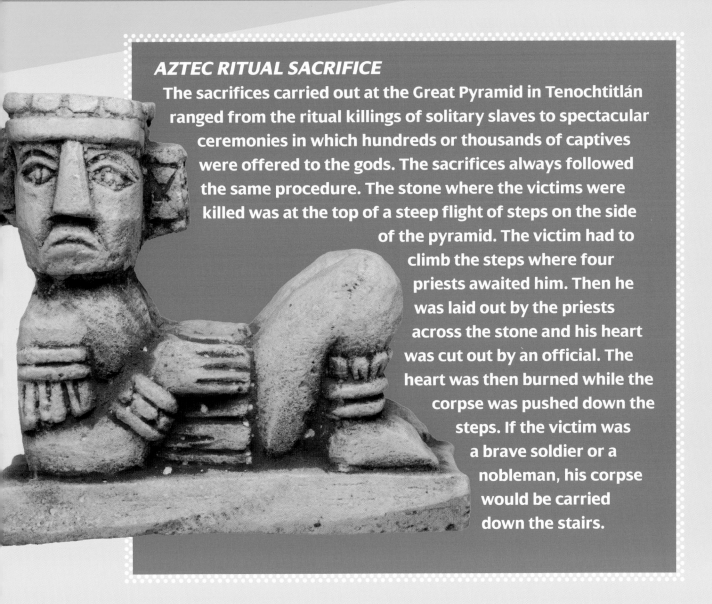

AZTEC RITUAL SACRIFICE

The sacrifices carried out at the Great Pyramid in Tenochtitlán ranged from the ritual killings of solitary slaves to spectacular ceremonies in which hundreds or thousands of captives were offered to the gods. The sacrifices always followed the same procedure. The stone where the victims were killed was at the top of a steep flight of steps on the side of the pyramid. The victim had to climb the steps where four priests awaited him. Then he was laid out by the priests across the stone and his heart was cut out by an official. The heart was then burned while the corpse was pushed down the steps. If the victim was a brave soldier or a nobleman, his corpse would be carried down the stairs.

on the battlefield and as a human sacrifice. It was to Huitzilopochtli, the god of war and sacrifice, that most offerings were made.

Aztec sacrifice reflected a general religious belief in Mesoamerica. It was based on the idea that the gods had willingly made sacrifices to create the world and humans, and it was, therefore, the responsibility of everyone on earth to repay the gods' sacrifice through their own human sacrifice. In addition, Mesoamericans believed that the gods, although supernatural, were mortal and so needed food to stay alive. The Mayas thought that ritual bloodletting was a good way of feeding the gods, because human blood was the best food available.

The Five Suns

The Aztecs believed there were four worlds, each with its own ruling sun, that preceded the current one. Each of the previous suns and worlds was dramatically destroyed by dueling gods.

In the beginning the Creator Couple, Tonacatecuhtli and Tonacacihuatl, gave birth to sons who battled with each other to create the heavens, the earth, the sea, the underworld, and fire. The sons also made the first humans and the calendar.

Tezcatlipoca, one of the sons, ruled over the first world, which was known as the Sun of the Earth. Giants roamed this world who were so strong that they could pull up trees with their bare hands. Quetzalcoatl, Tezcatlipoca's brother, punched him into the sea to get rid of him. But Tezcatlipoca rose out of the ocean and turned himself into a huge jaguar. When he returned to earth he brought many jaguars that ate the giants.

Another new world was created, known as the Sun of the Wind, with Quetzalcoatl as its ruler. Tezcatlipoca, who was still angry with Quetzalcoatl, hit him causing a huge wind that carried off Quetzalcoatl and all his creatures. The ones left became monkeys and swung high in the trees.

The third world, called the Sun of Rain, was ruled by Tlaloc, another son of the Creator Couple. But Quetzalcoatl destroyed the third world with fiery rain that poured down on all of Tlaloc's creatures, turning them into turkeys.

The fourth world was the Sun of Water. This world was ruled by Tlaloc's wife, Chalchiuhtlicue. This time Tezcatlipoca sent a great flood that washed away the mountains, causing the heavens to crash into the fourth world. At the same time, all of Chalchiuhtlicue's creatures were turned into fish.

The Fifth World

After the end of the fourth world, the gods decided that the fifth world should be created by one of them sacrificing himself in a bonfire. The first god to volunteer was the proud and rich Tecuciztecatl. But the other gods wanted to sacrifice Nanahuatzin, a poor and sick god whose body was covered in sores.

On the appointed day, Tecuciztecatl ran toward the fire and stopped as he felt the heat. Three more times he tried to jump in and failed. Then it was Nanahuatzin's turn. The poor god jumped into the flames at the first try and became the fifth sun, known as Nahui Ollin, which shone brightly over the new earth. Tecuciztecatl was so ashamed that he jumped in after Nanahuatzin and became the moon.

In the center of this early Aztec calendar disk is an image of the face of Nanahuatzin, who sacrificed himself to become the sun god Nahui Ollin.

Aztec Calendars

The Aztecs developed complex calendars for predicting seasonal changes, which was vitally important to farming. They also used the calendars to forecast sacred periods of danger.

In the National Museum of Anthropology in Mexico City stands the Sun Stone, or Aztec calendar, a large round stone covered with intricate carvings. In the center of the stone is an image of Nahui Ollin, the current sun, which was created when the god Nanahuatzin threw himself into the fire. Around him are the names of the four earlier suns, as told in "The Five Suns" myth (see page 38).

The Aztecs used the day and night skies as the basis for two methods of keeping track of the year. The first method, based on a Mayan calendar, had a 260-day cycle, made up of units of 20 consecutive days. Each 20-day period was named for a deity and combined with numbers from 1 to 13. A whole cycle was completed when every name and number combination, such as Tlaloc 3 or Huitzilopochtli 12, had passed.

The second type of calendar was based on the solar year and lasted for 365 days. It was made up of

This image of an Aztec calendar sun stone appears on some Mexican 500 peso bank bills.

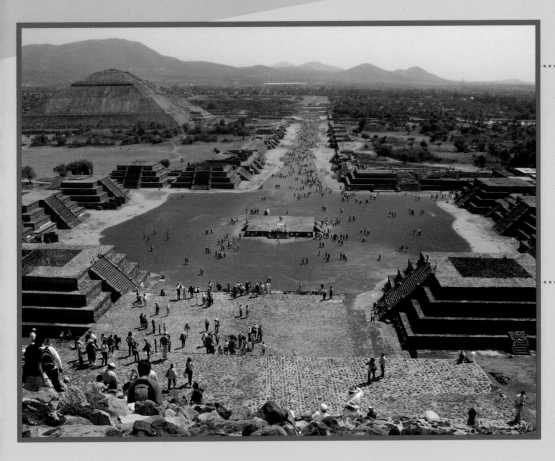

The pyramids in the city of Teotihuacan in Mexico are dedicated to the sun and the moon.

18 periods of 20 days, with five spare days at the end of the year.

Avoiding Destruction

The Aztecs believed that, when the calendars aligned, every 52 years, the world was threatened with destruction. Therefore, it was important to mark the end of a 52-year period with rituals involving the whole community. If these rituals were not followed correctly, the gods might then destroy everything.

To appease the gods, each cycle ended with a New Fire Ceremony. For five days before the end of the cycle, altar fires were extinguished, and people destroyed their furniture and possessions as they mourned the passing of the old cycle.

On the last day of the cycle, priests traveled to the Hill of the Star, a crater in the Valley of Mexico, to wait for the Pleiades, or Seven Sisters, to appear in the night sky. If the stars were visible, the world would continue. To celebrate, the priests lit a fire in the body of a dead animal from which all other fires were lit. Sacrifices, feasting, and the renovating of people's possessions would follow.

The Departure of Quetzalcoatl

The myth of Tezcatlipoca's victory over Quetzalcoatl is symbolic of the historic victory, long before the Aztecs, of the aggressive Toltec culture over the peaceful Teotihuacans.

When Quetzalcoatl ruled over the Toltecs they were happy. They were skilled at crafts and Tula, their capital city, grew rich. As the years passed, Quetzalcoatl grew old and ill, and it was then that Tezcatlipoca, who had been waiting for an opportunity to get rid of his rival Quetzalcoatl, began his evil tricks.

Disguised as an old man, Tezcatlipoca presented himself at the royal palace in Tula and told the guards he had medicine for their ruler. Quetzalcoatl received the old man, but when he was offered the medicine, he recognized Tezcatlipoca. Discovered, Tezcatlipoca fled.

Within a few days, Tezcatlipoca returned to Tula, this time disguised as a seller of green chilies. He stood near the palace until Quetzalcoatl's daughter noticed him. On first sight she fell passionately in love with the chili seller. She pleaded with her father to let her marry him and, not realizing that the chili seller was really Tezcatlipoca, Quetzalcoatl consented.

Evil Influence

Following the marriage Tezcatlipoca, as the chili seller, started to exert a strong power over the Toltecs, causing a series of disasters. First he hypnotized a large group of people with his singing. Then, beating a drum faster and faster, he led the people dancing over the edge of a ravine, where they were turned to stone.

Other disasters followed until one day he caused all the food in Tula to rot. Following this, Tezcatlipoca disguised himself as an old woman and started to roast fresh corn. Lured by the smell, the remaining Toltecs rushed to the old woman's house. As soon as they entered, Tezcatlipoca killed them.

With the Toltecs dead, Quetzalcoatl knew that the time had come for him to leave Tula. He set fire to the city, buried his silver and gold, ordered all the brightly colored birds to fly away, and changed the cacao trees into worthless cacti. Then he left, accompanied by his faithful dwarfs and hunchbacks.

Quetzalcoatl and his entourage walked many miles to the east. When asked where he was going, he replied, "I am going to learn."

But Tezcatlipoca was not satisfied with expelling Quetzalcoatl from Tula and continued to chase him. As Quetzalcoatl and his group climbed the snowy slopes of the volcanoes of Popocatepetl and Ixtaccihuatl, all his companions died of cold and Quetzalcoatl was left alone.

When Quetzalcoatl reached the sea, he used the only magical power he had left and made a raft out of serpents, on which he sailed away to an unknown destination.

This is one of the ornamental masks on the walls of the Temple of Quetzalcoatl at Teotihuacan.

The Fall of the Aztec Empire

Ruthless and fearsome, the Aztec empire ruled neighboring cultures with a heavy hand. Yet within a matter of months, a small band of Spanish soldiers destroyed the mighty empire.

The belief that the mythical god Quetzalcoatl would return played a crucial role in the downfall of the Aztec empire. Since 1502, when Montezuma II was crowned ruler of the Aztecs, there had been a series of strange omens. These included a comet in the night sky and soothsayers having visions of the destruction of the Aztec capital, Tenochtitlán.

Then, in April 1519, a white, bearded warrior wearing a hat with plumed feathers anchored his ship and set up camp near modern-day Veracruz. To many throughout the empire, this stranger was the Toltec god Quetzalcoatl—often represented as a plumed serpent—returning to reclaim his place as ruler of the Toltecs and Aztecs.

In fact, the white, bearded warrior was the conquistador Hernando Cortés, who had come to the New World to expand Spanish territories and to search for gold.

Montezuma II sent gifts of jewels, gold, and human sacrifices in an attempt to persuade Cortés to stay

This painting is an artist's impression of the death of Montezuma II, the last emperor of the Aztecs.

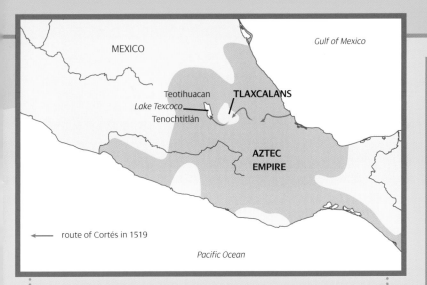

This map shows the Aztec empire at the time of the arrival of the conquistadores.

This Spanish painting depicts Mexico City at the start of the sixteenth century.

away from Tenochtitlán. Cortés, however, had already learned that he had been mistaken for Quetzalcoatl. He began marching his troops toward the Aztec capital.

Besieging Tenochtitlán

Although he had only a few hundred soldiers, compared to the millions of Aztecs, Cortés did have several advantages. Unlike the Aztecs, the conquistadores had horses, guns, and well-trained fighters. Also, during his march to Tenochtitlán he formed alliances with Mesoamerican tribes, such as the Tlaxcalans, who were hostile to the Aztecs.

When the Spanish arrived at Tenochtitlán on November 8, 1519, they were welcomed as guests but quickly betrayed the Aztec emperor's trust by taking him prisoner. In July 1520, during an Aztec counterattack, Montezuma II was killed either by his own warriors or strangled by the Spanish. Tenochtitlán finally surrendered in August 1521.

END OF THE AZTECS

During the hundred years after the capture of Tenochtitlán, the Aztec population fell from an estimated 12 million to a few hundred thousand. The decrease was due mostly to diseases such as smallpox, measles, and typhus, to which the Aztecs had no immunity. Many of the survivors married Spanish settlers, and the Aztecs ceased to be a distinct people.

Glossary

ayllu An Inca social group to which members were loyal. Every member of the Inca empire belonged to an ayllu.

Cavillaca In an Inca myth, a woman who fled to the sea when she discovered that the spirit Coniraya Viracocha was the father of her baby. When she reached the sea, she and her baby turned into rocks.

Chalchiuhtlicue The wife of the god Tlaloc. In an Aztec myth, she ruled over the fourth world, known as the Sun of Water.

Chichén Itzá One of the major Mayan cities on the Yucatán Peninsula of Mexico.

codex An ancient manuscript, usually with illustrated pages.

Coniraya Viracocha An Inca spirit who tricked a beautiful woman into having his child. His actions delivered fish to the sea.

conquistador Meaning "one who conquers," a leader of Spanish troops in the conquest of Mesoamerica and Peru.

Cortés, Hernando Born in 1485 and died in 1547, the Spanish conquistador who conquered the Aztec empire.

Coyolxauhqui The warrior goddess who tried to kill her mother, Coatlicue, and was defeated by her brother Huitzilopochtli.

Cuzco The capital of the Inca empire. According to legend, it was founded by Manco Capac and his sister Mama Ocllo. The ancient city is located in Peru.

floating gardens Gardens built by the Aztecs for farming; they floated atop Lake Texcoco in Mexico.

Gucumatz In a Mayan myth, he was a plumed serpent who, along with the god Huracan, made the corn people, ancestors of humans.

hieroglyphics A system of writing that is made up mostly of drawings or illustrations instead of letters.

Huitzilopochtli Aztec god of war.

Hunahpu In Mayan mythology, Hunahpu and his twin brother, Xbalanque, defeated the evil lords of Xibalba and destroyed the bird god Vucub Caquix.

Huracan The Mayan sky god who, with Gucumatz, made the corn people, the ancestors of humans.

Mama Ocllo The sister of Manco Capac who, with her brother, founded Cuzco.

Manco Capac The first ruler (or Inca) of the Quechua speakers.

Mesoamerica During pre-Columbian times, it was the region that spread from modern-day central Mexico to Nicaragua.

mita A tax, usually in the form of weapons, cloth, potatoes, or corn, that most members of the Inca empire were forced to pay.

Mixtecs A Mesoamerican civilization that was conquered by the Aztecs in the fifteenth century.

Montezuma II Born in 1466 and died in 1520, thought of as the last Aztec ruler. He was captured by Cortés and killed by either Spanish soldiers or Aztec warriors.

Nanahuatzin A sickly Aztec god who became the fifth sun and was then known as Nahui Ollin.

New Fire Ceremony An Aztec ritual held every 52 years to mark the end of the sacred cycle. During the ceremony, the Aztecs burned all their belongings.

Olmecs The first great civilization in Mesoamerica, where they were dominant from 1100 B.C. to 800 B.C.

Pachacuti Inca ruler during the fifteenth century who greatly expanded the empire.

Popol Vuh A book of Mayan mythology from the sixteenth century.

pre-Columbian Refers to the period before the European explorer Christopher Columbus arrived in the so-called New World.

Quechua The language spoken by the Incas. Scholars generally refer to the Incas as the Quechua speakers.

Quetzalcoatl Originally a Teotihuacan deity, later adopted by the Toltecs and the Aztecs. He was often represented as a feathered serpent.

slash-and-burn farming The practice of cutting down and burning forests and vegetation to make way for farmland. It was used by the Mayas in Yucatán.

Sun Stone An ancient Aztec calendar now housed in a museum in Mexico City.

Tecuciztecatl An Aztec god who wanted to be the fifth sun, Nahui Ollin, but instead became the moon.

Tenochtitlán The capital of the Aztec empire. The city, which lies beneath modern Mexico City, was founded in around A.D. 1325. The god Huitzilopochtli supposedly guided the ancient Aztecs to the site of Tenochtitlán.

terrace farming The practice of carving out level terraces in the side of a steep mountain for farming.

Tezcatlipoca An Aztec deity who was usually described as the enemy of Quetzalcoatl.

tlachtli The ancient Mesoamerican ball game, which was played similarly to modern basketball or soccer.

Tlaloc Originally an Olmec deity who was adopted by the Aztecs as their god of rain.

Tlaltecuhtli A greedy female Aztec monster whose dismembered body became the earth.

Tlaxcalans Enemies of the Aztecs who helped Hernando Cortés conquer Tenochtitlán in the sixteenth century.

Toltecs Ancient civilization that dominated Mesoamerica between the eras of the Olmecs and the Aztecs.

Tula Ancient capital city of the Toltec empire.

Viracocha According to the Incas, the supreme being and the driving force behind all creation.

Vucub Caquix The boastful bird god of the Mayas who threatened the creation of humans.

Xbalanque The brother of the Mayan hero Hunahpu.

Xibalba In Mayan mythology, the kingdom of the underworld.

Xiuhcoatl A serpent of fire that was used as a weapon by the Aztec god Huitzilopochtli to defeat his warrior sister Coyolxauhqui.

Further Information

BOOKS
Ardagh, Philip. *History Detectives: Aztecs*. New York, NY: Peter Bedrick Books, 2000.

Baquedano, Elizabeth. *Eyewitness: Aztec, Inca, and Maya*. New York, NY: Dorling Kindersley Publishing, 2000.

Drew, David. *Early Civilization Series: Inca Life*. Hauppauge, NY: Barrons Juveniles, 2000.

Florescano, Enrique (translated by Lysa Hochroth). *The Myth of Quetzalcoatl*. Baltimore, MD: Johns Hopkins University Press, 1999.

Ganeri, Anita. *Mesoamerican Myth: A Treasury of Central American Legends, Art, and History*. Armonk, NY: Sharpe Focus, 2008.

McManus, Kay. *Land of the Five Suns: Looking at Aztec Myths and Legends*. Lincolnwood, IL: NTC Publishing Group, 1997.

Nicholson, Sue. *Aztecs and Incas: A Guide to the Pre-Colonized Americas in 1504*. New York, NY: Larousse Kingfisher Chambers, 2000.

VIDEOS
Great Cities of the World: Fall of the Aztec and Maya Empires. Questar, 1999.

Lost Mummies of the Inca. A&E Video, 2000.

National Geographic's Lost Kingdoms of the Maya. National Geographic, 1997.

Nova: Secrets of Lost Empires—Inca. WGBH Boston, 1997.

WEB SITES
Ancient Mesoamerican Civilizations
   http://www.angelfire.com/ca/humanorigins

Ancient Web: Ancient Mexico
   http://www.theancientweb.com/explore/content.aspx?content_id=19

Encyclopedia Mythica: An Encyclopedia on Mythology, Folklore, and Legend
   http://www.pantheon.org/mythica

Index

Page numbers in *italics* refer to picture captions

Andes Mountains 4, 5, 13, *19*
Atahualpa *17*
Ayar Cachi 18
Ayar Manco 18
Ayar Sauca 18
Ayar Ucho 18
ayllu 17
Aztec calendar 40
Aztecs 5, *7*, 8, 9, 13, 25, 30,
   32, *33*, 34, *35*, 36–37, 38, *39*,
   40–41, 42, 44–45

Bonampak 29

Cabraca 26
cacao 43
cactus, cacti 32, 43
calendars 5, 40–41
Cavillaca 14
Chalchiuhtlicue 38
Chiapas 29
Chichén Itzá 25, 29, *31*
Chile 9
Coatepec 30
Coatlicue 30, 31
Coba, Mexico *24*
codex *see* codices
codices 28
condor 14
Coniraya Viracocha 14–15, 16
conquistadores 44, 45
Copán 29
corn 11, 12, 13, 17, 26, 34, 42
corn people 10–11
Cortés, Hernando 44, 45
Coyolxauhqui 30, 31
crab 27
crops 12, 13
Cuzco 9, 18–19, 20–21

death mask *8*

eagle 32
Ecuador 9

farming 13
fish 15, 38
floating gardens 13
fox 14

gesso 28
gold 44
Great Pyramid 32, 33, 37
Gucumatz 10, 11
gypsum 28

hieroglyphics 5, 28
Hill of the Star 41
Honduras 12, 29
Huanacauri 18
Huitzilpochtli 9, 30–31, 32–33,
   37, 40
Hunahpu 22, 24, 26, 27, 28
Hunhun-Ahpu 22
Huracan 10, 11

Incas 8, 9, *12*, 13, 16–17, 19, 20–21
Ixtaccihuatl 43

jaguars 33, 38

macaws 14, 15, 29
Machu Picchu *17*
Mama Ocllo 18, 19
Manco Capac 19, 20
Mayas 5, 8, *23*, 24–25, 26,
   27, 28–29, 37
Mayan calendar 40
Mayan gods 9, *11*
measles 45
Mexico 5, 7, 8, 9, 12, *31*, *41*
Mexico City 32, *33*, 40, *45*
mita 17
mixtamal 12

Mixtecs 4, 8
monkey 38
Montezuma II 44, 45
murals 29

Nahui Ollin 39, 40
Nanahuatzin 38, 39, 40
New Fire Ceremony 41
Nicaragua 12

Olmecs 4, 8, 24

Pachacuti 20
Paqaritampu, Mount 18
Peru *17*, *19*, *21*
Pleiades 41
Popocatepetl 43
Popol Vuh 26, 28
pre-Columbian 10, 12
puma 20

Quechua 20
Quetzalcoatl 6, 7, 9, 34, 38,
   42–43, 44
Quetzalpetatl 34

sacrifice, human 32, 36–37
serpents 32, 43
Seven Sisters *see* Pleiades
slash-and-burn farming 13
smallpox 45
Spanish 4, 5, 8, *13*, *21*, 44, 45
suns 38–39, 40
Sun Stone 40

Tecuciztecatl 38, 39
Temple of Jaguars 29
Temple of Quetzalcoatl *43*
Temple of the Sun 21
Tenochtitlán 9, 13, 32, 37,
   44, 45
Teotihuacan *7*, *9*, *41*, *43*

Teotihuacans 4
terraces *12*, 13
Texcoco, Lake 13, 32
Tezcatlipoca 6, 7, 34, 38, 42, 43
tlachtli 22, 24–25
Tlaloc 9, 38, 40
Tlaltecuhtli 6, 7
Toltecs 8, 25, 30, 34, 42, 43, 44
Tonacacihuatl 38
Tonacatecuhtli 38
Tula 30, 42, 43
typhus 45

Valley of Mexico 41
Veracruz 44
Viarcocha 16, 18, 19
Vucub Caquix 26–27, 28, 29
Vucub-Ahpu 22

Wars of the Flowers, The 36

Xbalanque 22, 24, 26, 27, 28
Xibalba 22, 23
Xiuhcoatl 31
Xquiq 22

Yucatán 8, 13, 25

Zipacna 26, 27